I CAN DRAW

HORSES

I CAN DRAW

HORSES

BY GILL SPEIRS

A Little Simon Book
Published by Simon & Schuster, Inc., New York

Copyright © 1983 by Simon & Schuster, Inc.
All rights reserved
including the right of reproduction
in whole or in part in any form
Published by LITTLE SIMON
A Division of Simon & Schuster, Inc.
Simon & Schuster Building
1230 Avenue of the Americas
New York, New York 10020

Designed by Gil Speirs.

Manufactured in the United States of America
10 9 8 7 6 5

LITTLE SIMON and colophon are trademarks of Simon & Schuster, Inc.

Library of Congress Cataloging in Publication Data

Speirs, Gill.
I can draw horses.

(I can draw)
Summary: Give instructions on how to draw horses.
1. Horses in art—Juvenile literature. 2. Drawing—
Technique—Juvenile literature. [1. Horses in art,
2. Drawing—Technique] I. Title. II. Series.
NC783.8.H65S63   1983   743'.69725   82-25970
ISBN 0-671-46447-7

HERE'S HOW

Throughout this book simple shapes—squares, circles, ovals, rectangles, and triangles—are used to build up the basic form of the horse.

Draw these shapes over and over with free, bold lines until you can do them with ease. You will use them a lot as you work your way through the book.

The first drawing for each section will show you how to put the shapes together to make up the different parts of the horse.

These will help you to get to know the shape of the horse before following the step-by-step guides for your finished drawing.

Remember, the time to add the detail is when you feel the basic drawing is right.

As an extra bonus, this book includes a put-it-together-yourself model that you can move and pose to help you to create your very best horse drawings.

Don't be discouraged if you are not happy with the way your first drawings look. Practice. Draw as often as you can and you will soon develop the skills you need to draw the horse just the way you want.

GETTING STARTED

Looking and doing are the two best ways to learn to draw, whatever the subject may be. Use your eyes all the time to discover the shapes and forms of all you see around you.

Begin drawing on large sheets of paper. Use big lines to get the feeling of freedom and movement. Don't be afraid to draw with bold lines. If you make mistakes, you can always start again.

There are all sorts of pens, pencils, and crayons that you can use.

PENCILS can be soft or hard or anywhere in between. H pencils are hard, B pencils are soft. An HB pencil is good to start with. It will give you both soft lines and very fine lines if you keep it well sharpened.

CHARCOAL is very soft and black. It can be bought in sticks or in a pencil which is much easier to use. charcoal is useful for sketching. Smudging the line can be effective for shading areas of your drawing. But take care! You don't want smudges where they should not be.

PASTELS are similar in texture to charcoal but can be bought in lots of different colors.

PENS are quite versatile for drawing. Each type will give you a different kind of line. Crowquill and mapping pens are suitable for fine detailed drawing. Reed, bamboo, and quill pens make strong bold lines. Felt tip and fiber tip pens are the easiest to use. They are available in many widths, are very cheap and come in lots of colors. But they won't last long if you leave off their tops. So take care and put the tops on when you have finished using them.

Try out the various drawing materials. You will soon find which is your favorite.
Try them separately and together!

PARTS OF THE HORSE

Some parts of the horse have names you might not have heard before, but it is nice to know what you are drawing.

Try to learn the names of the different parts shown in the drawing so you will recognize them as you work your way through the book.

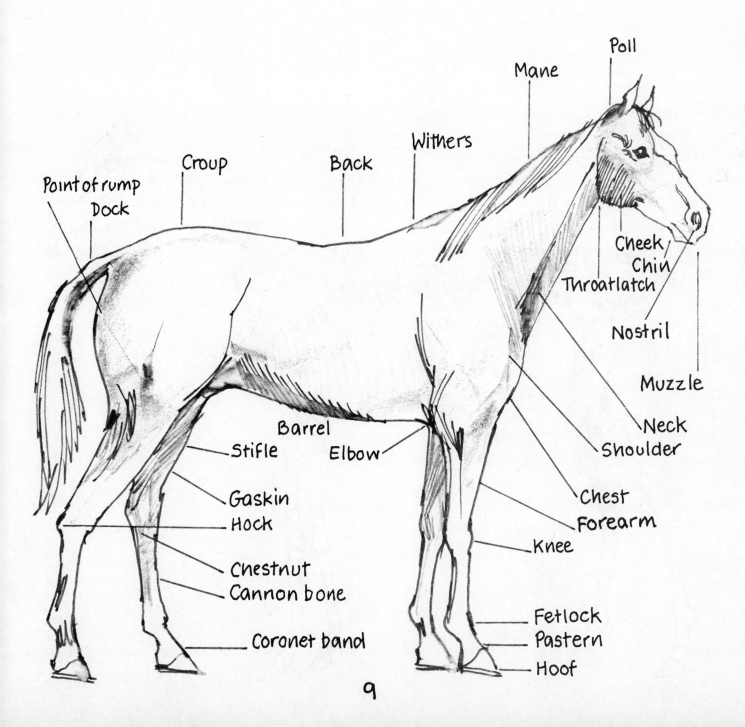

Poll

Mane

Withers

Croup

Back

Point of rump

Dock

Cheek

Chin

Throatlatch

Nostril

Muzzle

Neck

Shoulder

Barrel

Stifle

Elbow

Gaskin

Hock

Chest

Forearm

Knee

Chestnut

Cannon bone

Fetlock

Pastern

Coronet band

Hoof

THE SKELETON OF THE HORSE

Although you do not need to know the names of each of the bones and muscles that make up the horse, a study of the skeleton and muscular system will help you to understand how they relate to one another and to the overall shape of the horse.

Try always to be aware of the correct relative proportions of the horse in all your drawings.

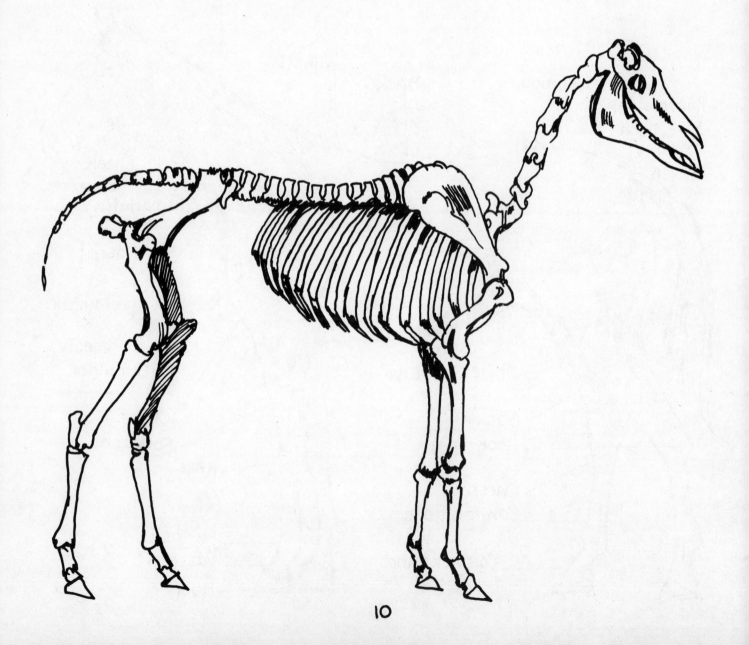

THE MUSCLES OF THE HORSE

This drawing shows how all the muscles build onto the skeleton to bring out the basic outer shape of the horse.

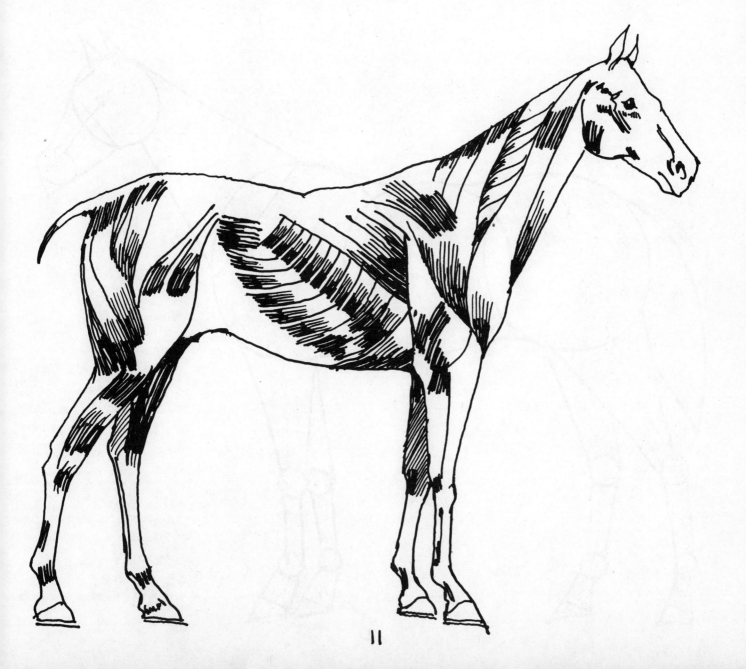

THE BASIC SHAPE

This drawing shows how the form of the horse can be broken down into very simple shapes — the circle, square, oval, rectangle, and triangle.

Practice drawing these shapes, and put them together as they are here to make your first, very simple drawing.

Illustrations on the following pages show how to draw horses from different points of view, each one starting in the easy-to-draw way shown on the next page.

EASY-TO-DRAW GUIDE

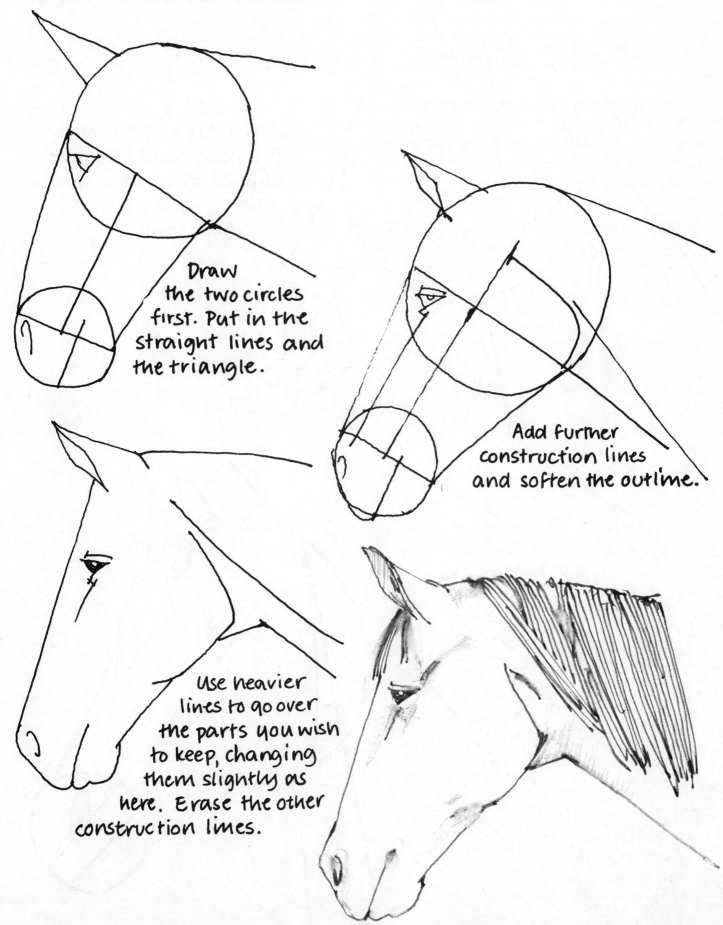

Draw the two circles first. Put in the straight lines and the triangle.

Add further construction lines and soften the outline.

Use heavier lines to go over the parts you wish to keep, changing them slightly as here. Erase the other construction lines.

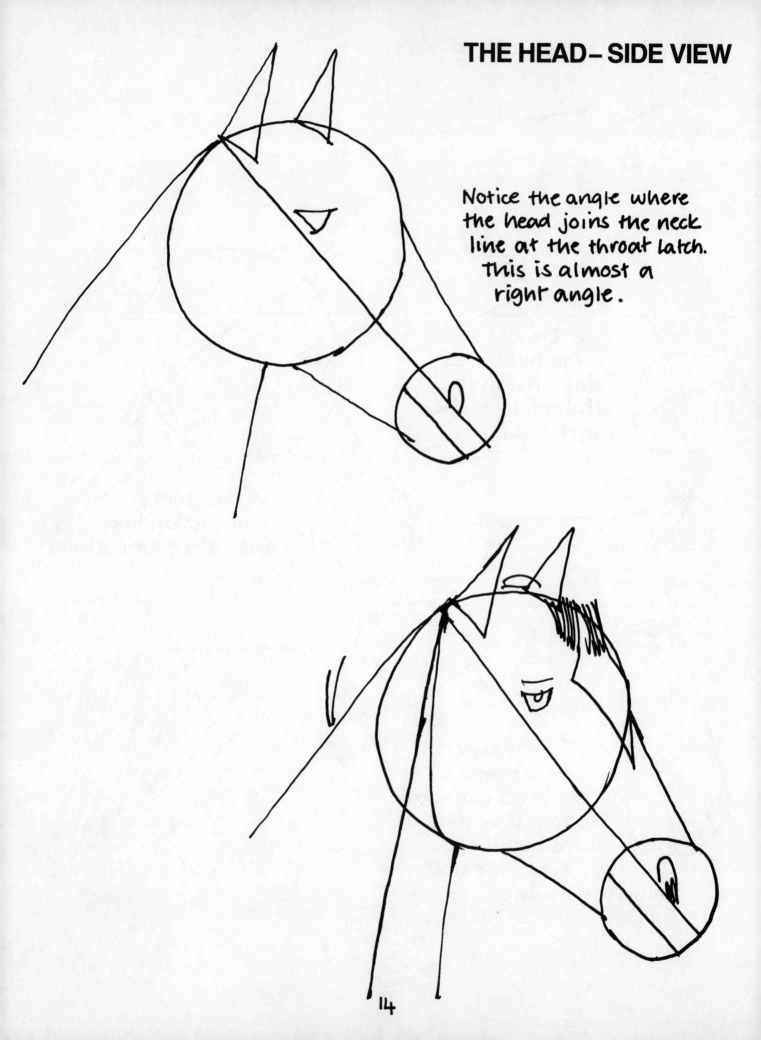

THE HEAD – SIDE VIEW

Notice the angle where the head joins the neck line at the throat latch. This is almost a right angle.

Remember, the head is a solid form. The shading and finishing details bring solidity and life to your drawing.

THE HEAD—FRONT VIEW

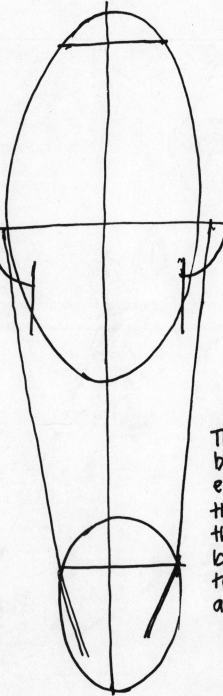

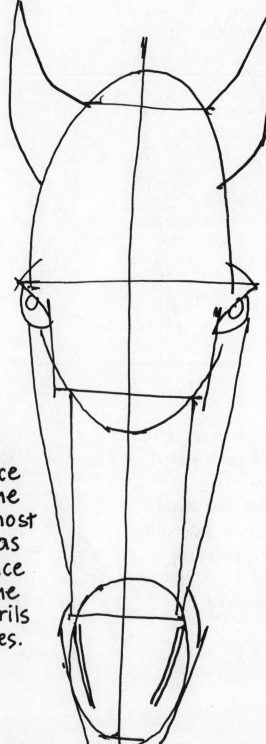

The distance between the eyes is almost the same as the distance between the top of nostrils and the eyes.

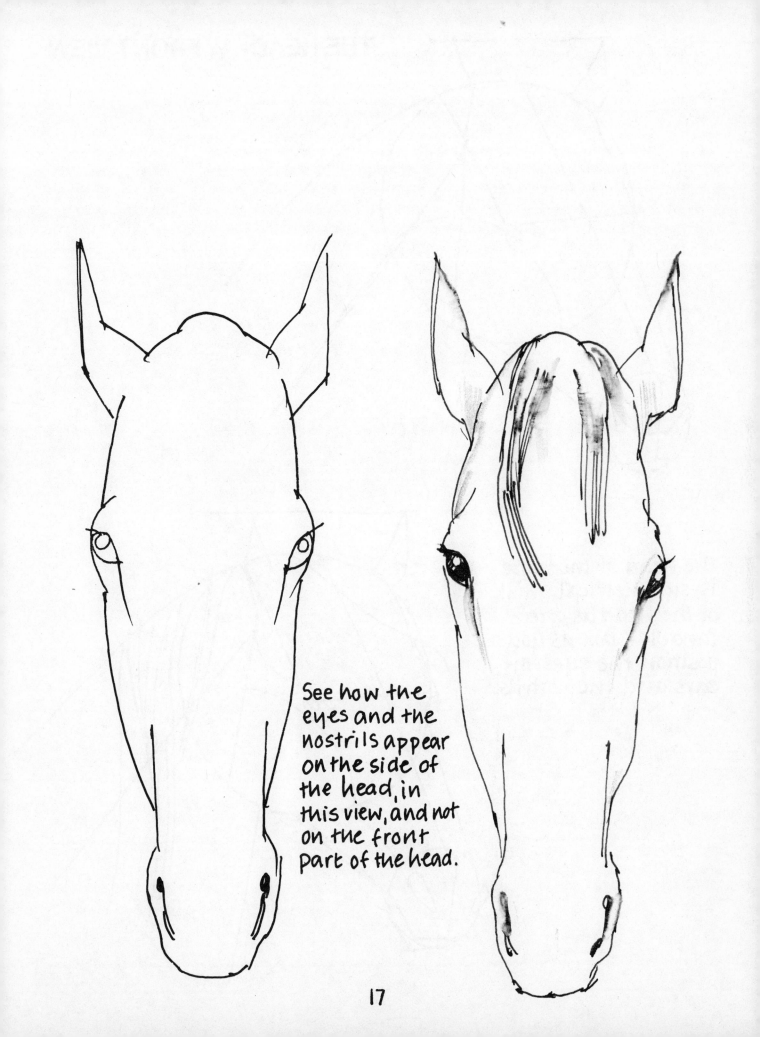

See how the eyes and the nostrils appear on the side of the head, in this view, and not on the front part of the head.

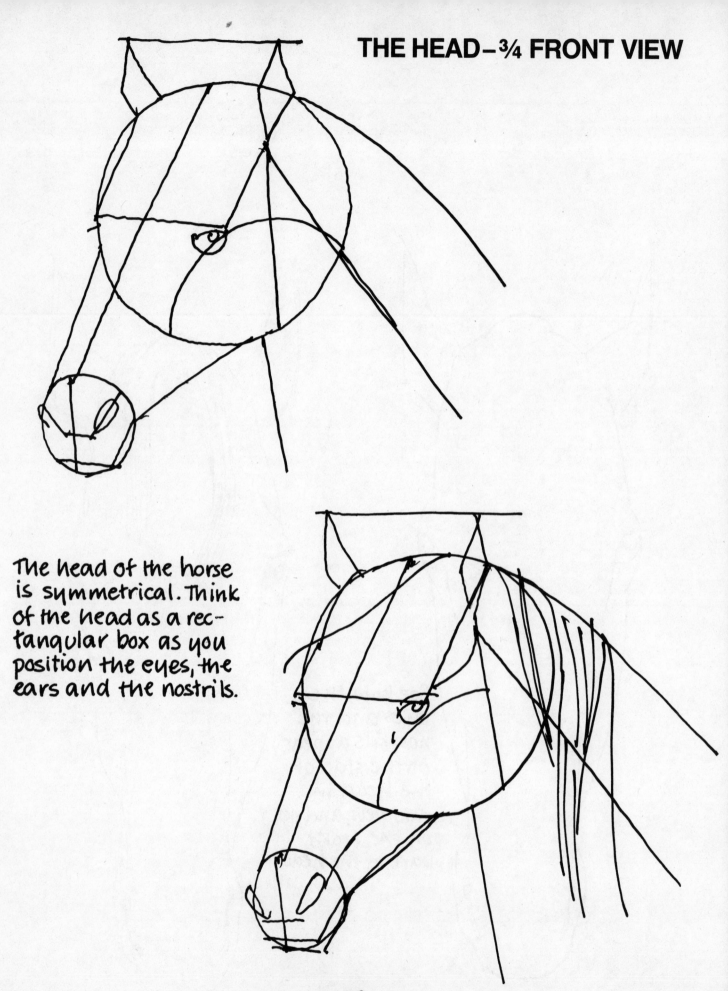

The head of the horse is symmetrical. Think of the head as a rectangular box as you position the eyes, the ears and the nostrils.

The ears appear to be almost funnel shaped.

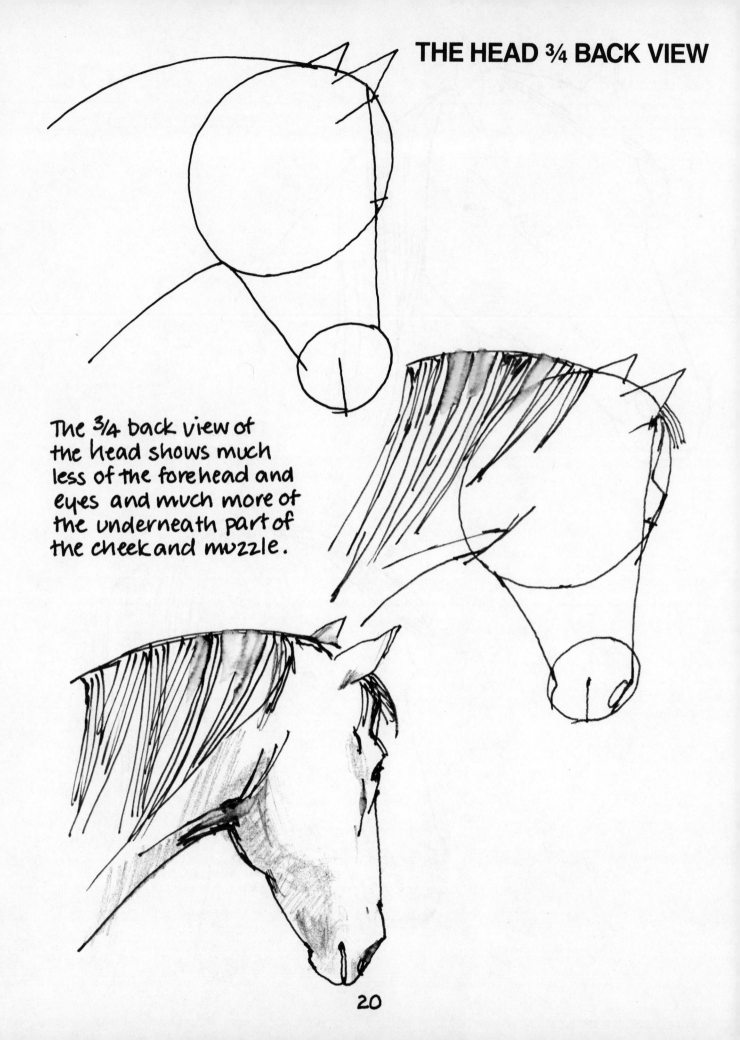

The ¾ back view of
the head shows much
less of the forehead and
eyes and much more of
the underneath part of
the cheek and muzzle.

The neck and head of the horse move in a gentle curve.

Here are some examples showing how the neck and head may look.

THE FULL BODY-SIDE VIEW

The whole body is drawn using simple steps in the same way you learned to draw the head.

Take care to get the proportions right. Although horses vary, the body and legs of the ideal horse fit neatly into a square.

The head extends beyond the square. Note how the top line of the neck is longer than the bottom line.

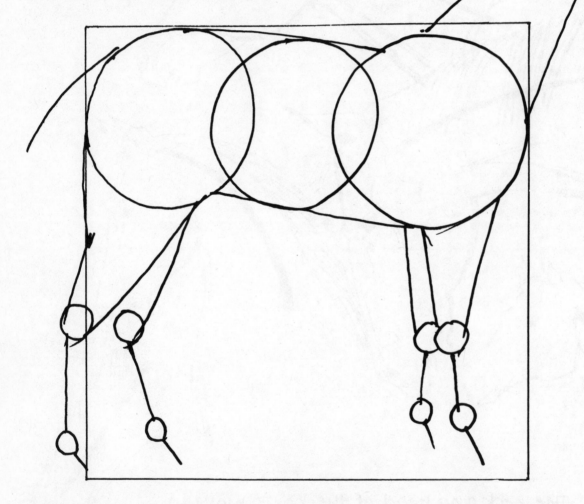

Notice how the length of leg relates to the body size.

Don't draw the head too small. The length of the head is the same as the distance between the front fetlock and the elbow.

See how the legs are placed to support the bulk of the body. The front legs are together and straight. The rear legs stand a little apart and are bent slightly at the hock.

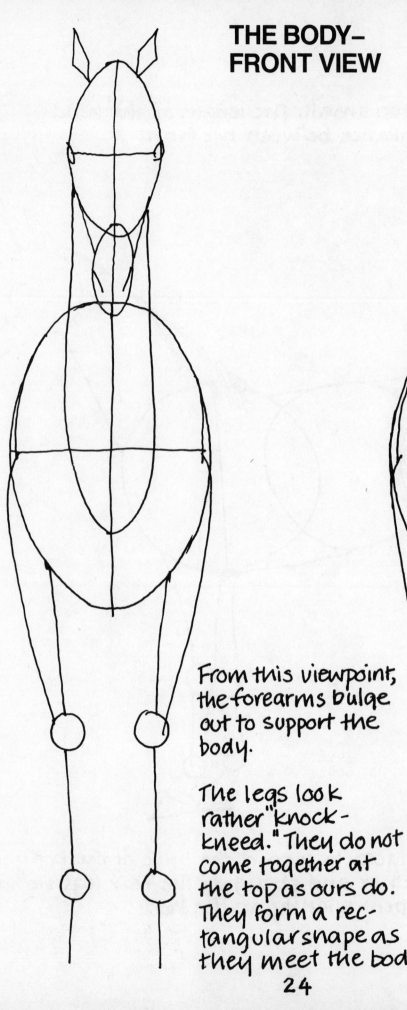

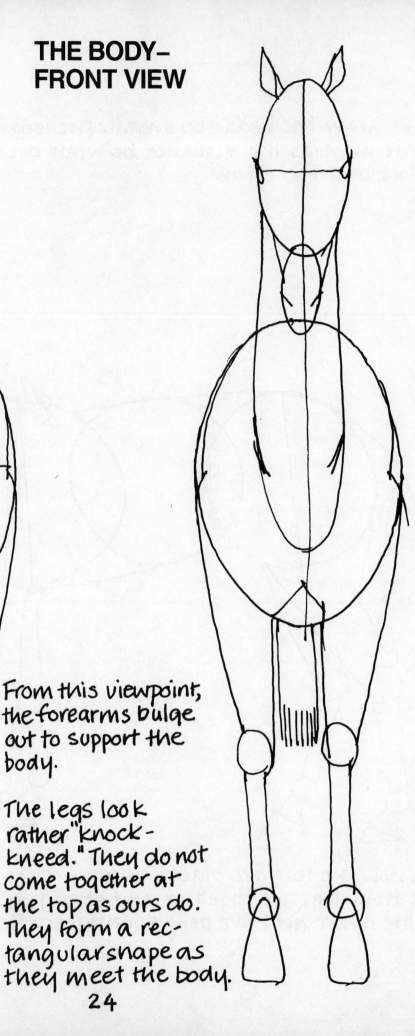

From this viewpoint, the forearms bulge out to support the body.

The legs look rather "knock-kneed." They do not come together at the top as ours do. They form a rectangular shape as they meet the body.

24

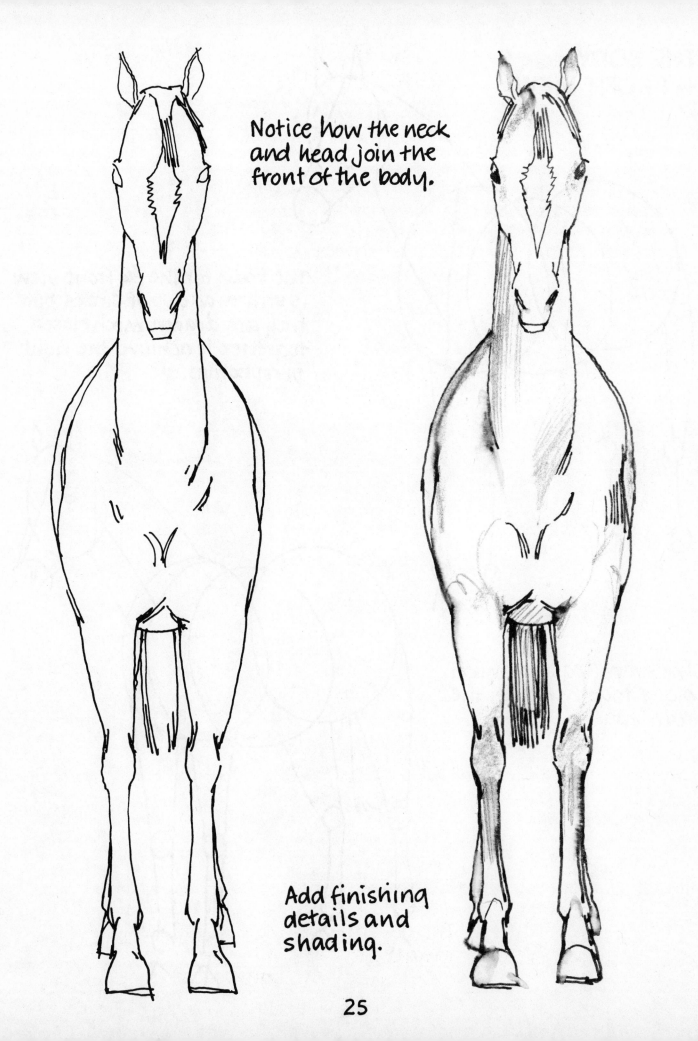

Notice how the neck
and head join the
front of the body.

Add finishing
details and
shading.

25

THE BODY— ¾ FRONT VIEW

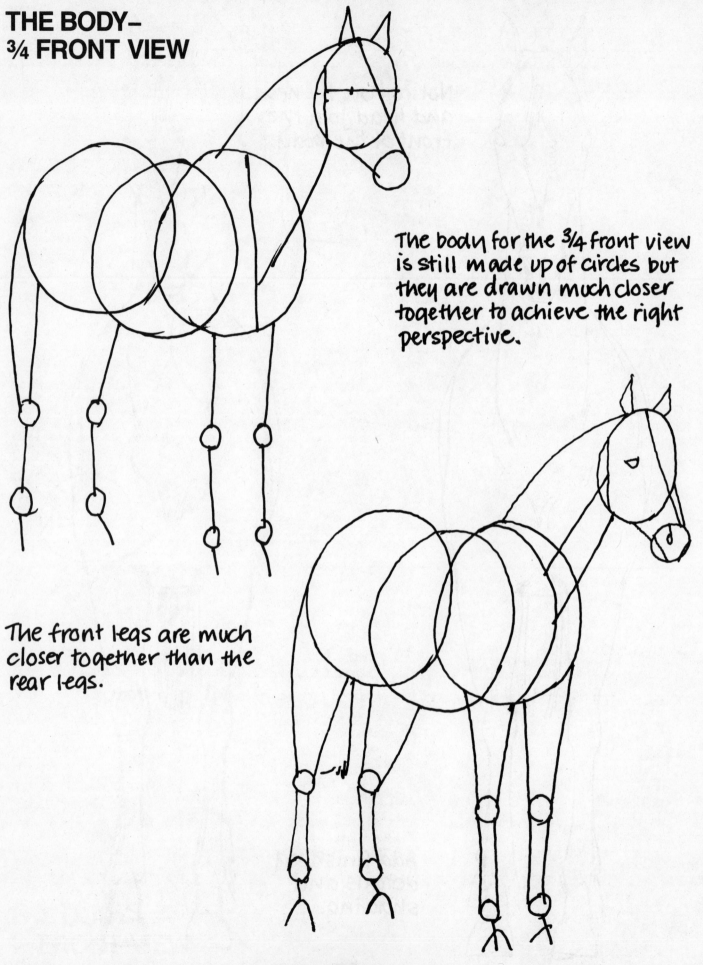

The body for the ¾ front view is still made up of circles but they are drawn much closer together to achieve the right perspective.

The front legs are much closer together than the rear legs.

26

THE BODY— ¾ BACK VIEW

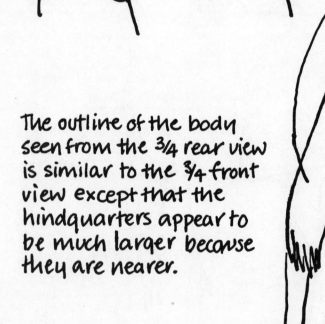

The outline of the body seen from the ¾ rear view is similar to the ¾ front view except that the hindquarters appear to be much larger because they are nearer.

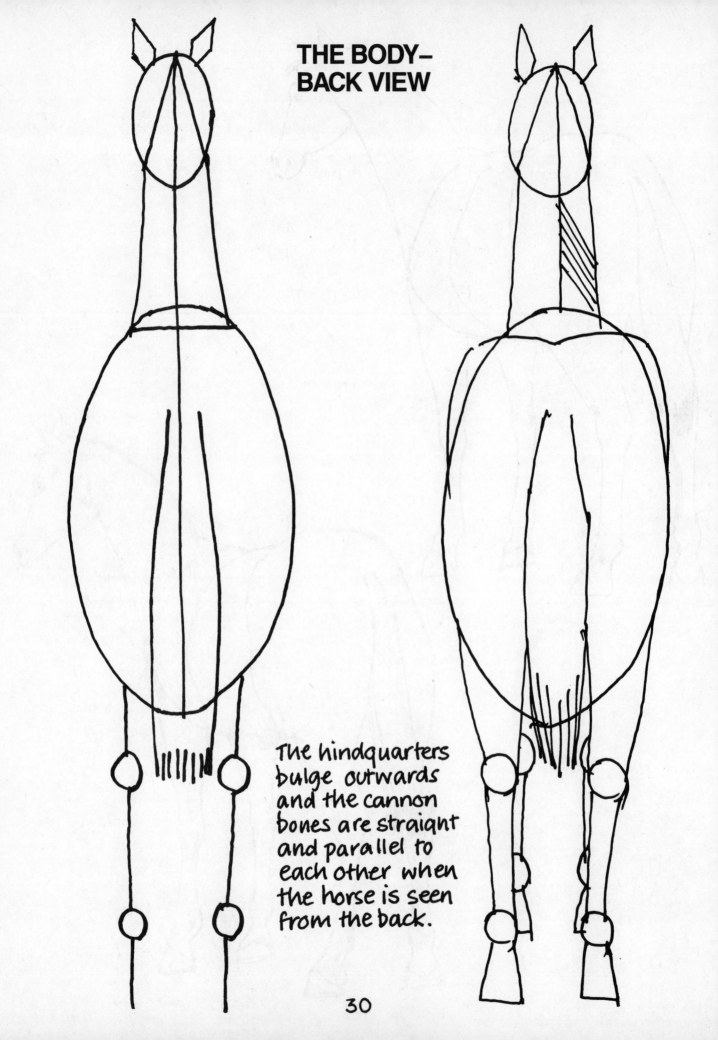

The hindquarters bulge outwards and the cannon bones are straignt and parallel to each other when the horse is seen from the back.

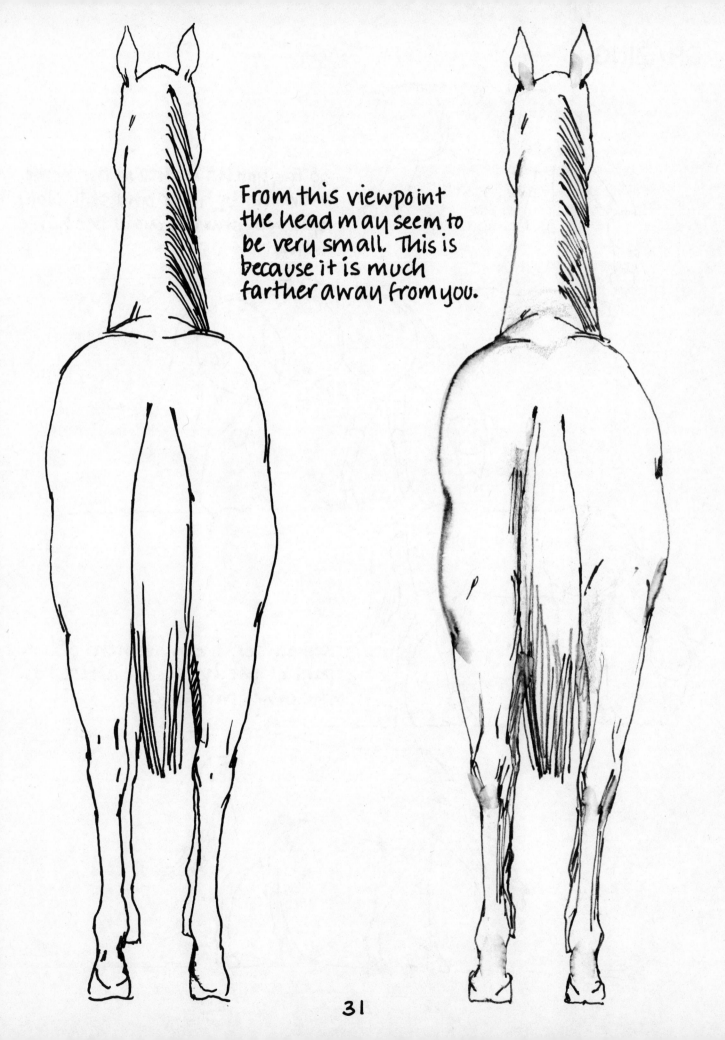

From this viewpoint
the head may seem to
be very small. This is
because it is much
farther away from you.

GRAZING

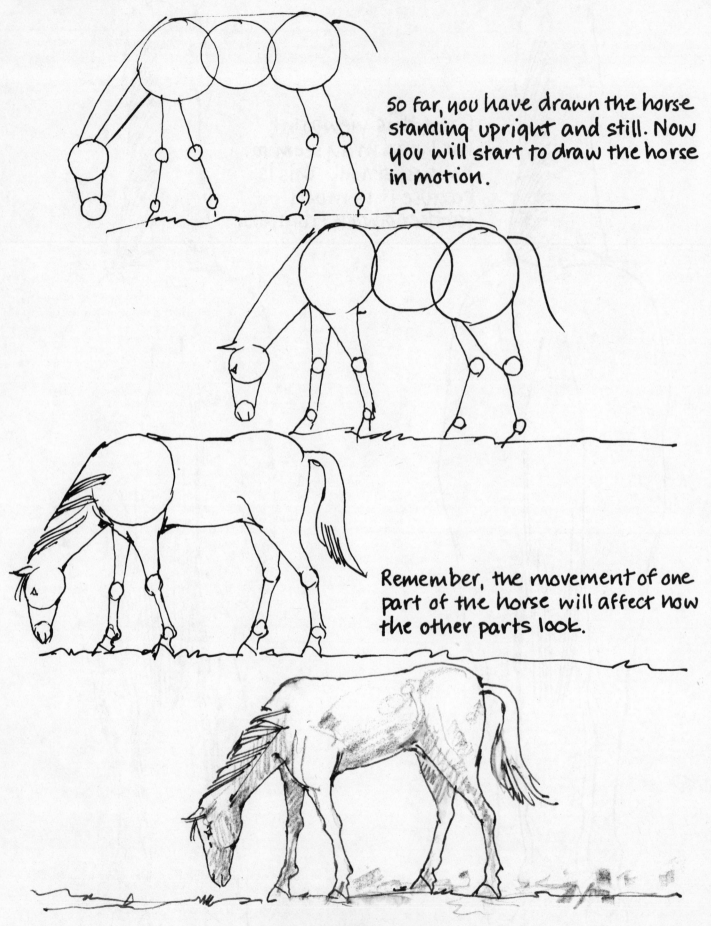

So far, you have drawn the horse standing upright and still. Now you will start to draw the horse in motion.

Remember, the movement of one part of the horse will affect how the other parts look.

32

Look carefully at the drawings on
the following pages to see where
the horses shape is changing as
he moves along.

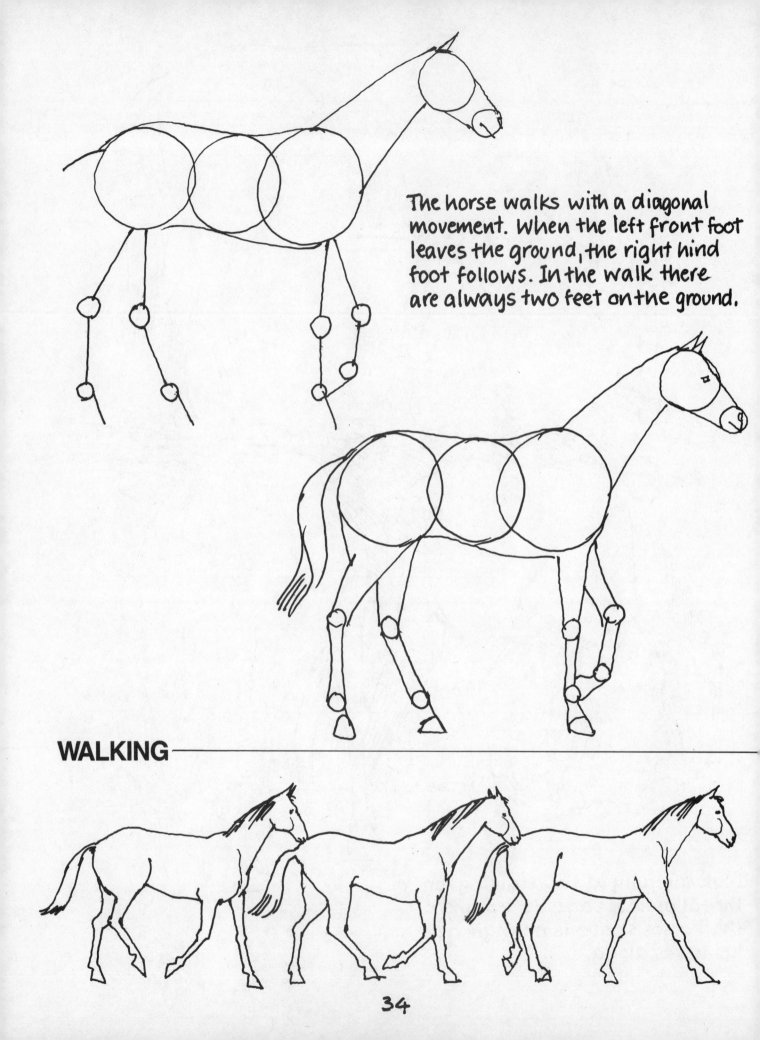

The horse walks with a diagonal movement. When the left front foot leaves the ground, the right hind foot follows. In the walk there are always two feet on the ground.

WALKING

Notice how the horse's
shoulders and hind-
quarters move along
with the legs.

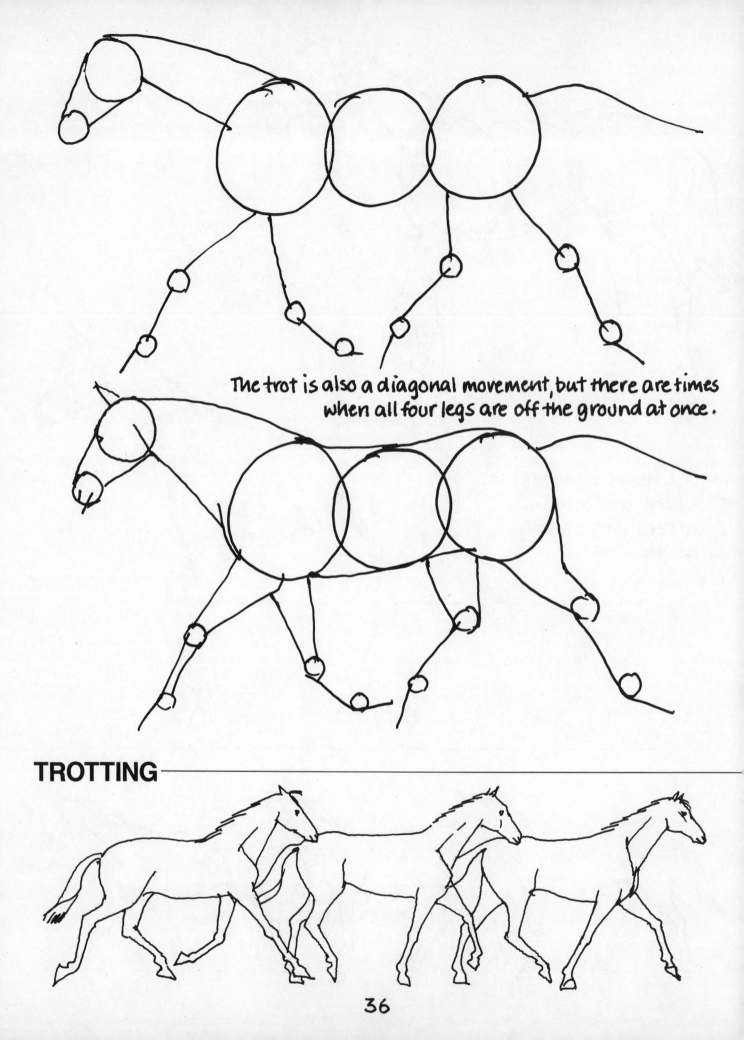

The trot is also a diagonal movement, but there are times when all four legs are off the ground at once.

TROTTING

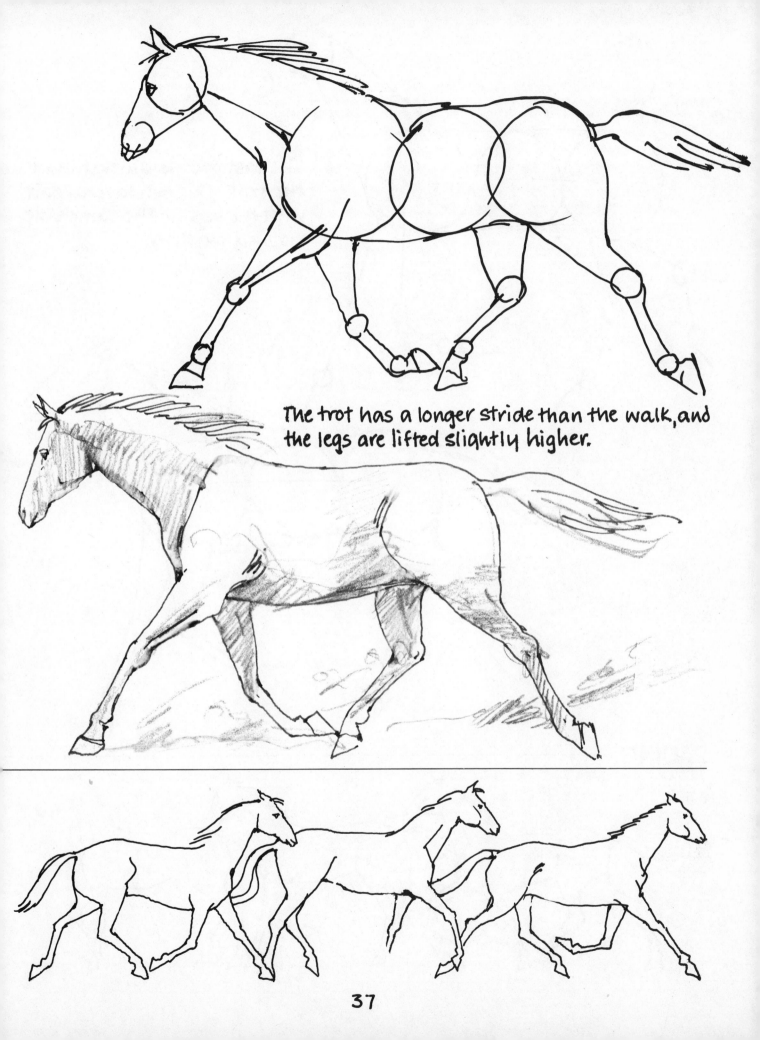

The trot has a longer stride than the walk, and the legs are lifted slightly higher.

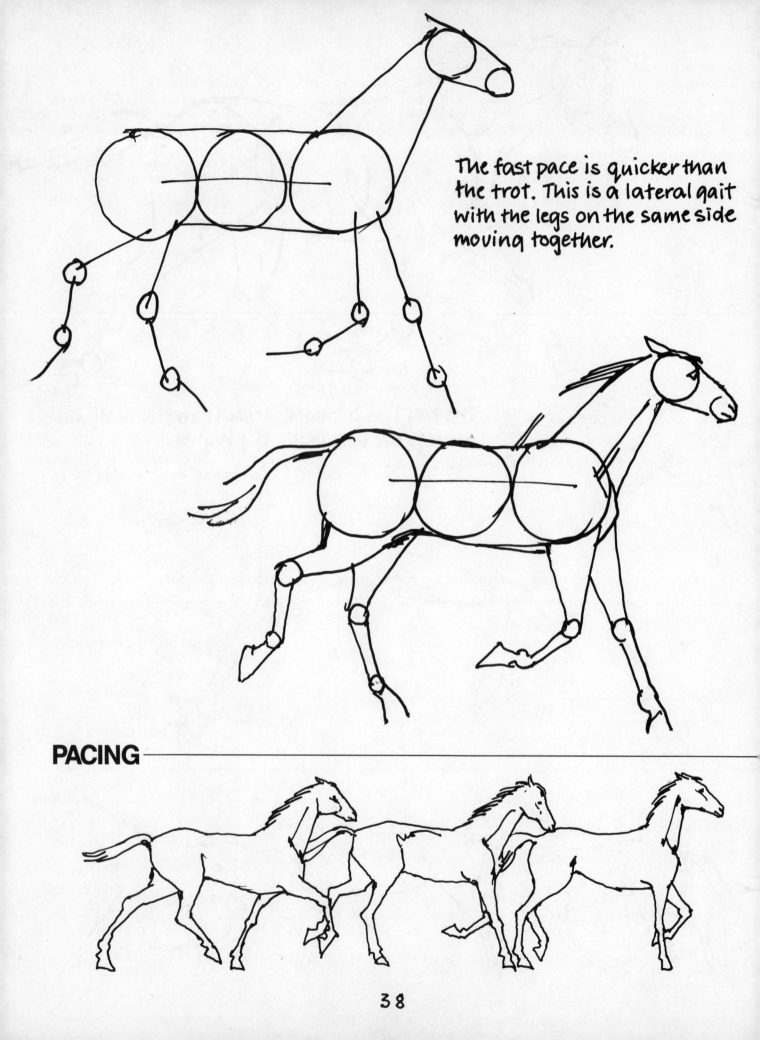

The fast pace is quicker than the trot. This is a lateral gait with the legs on the same side moving together.

PACING

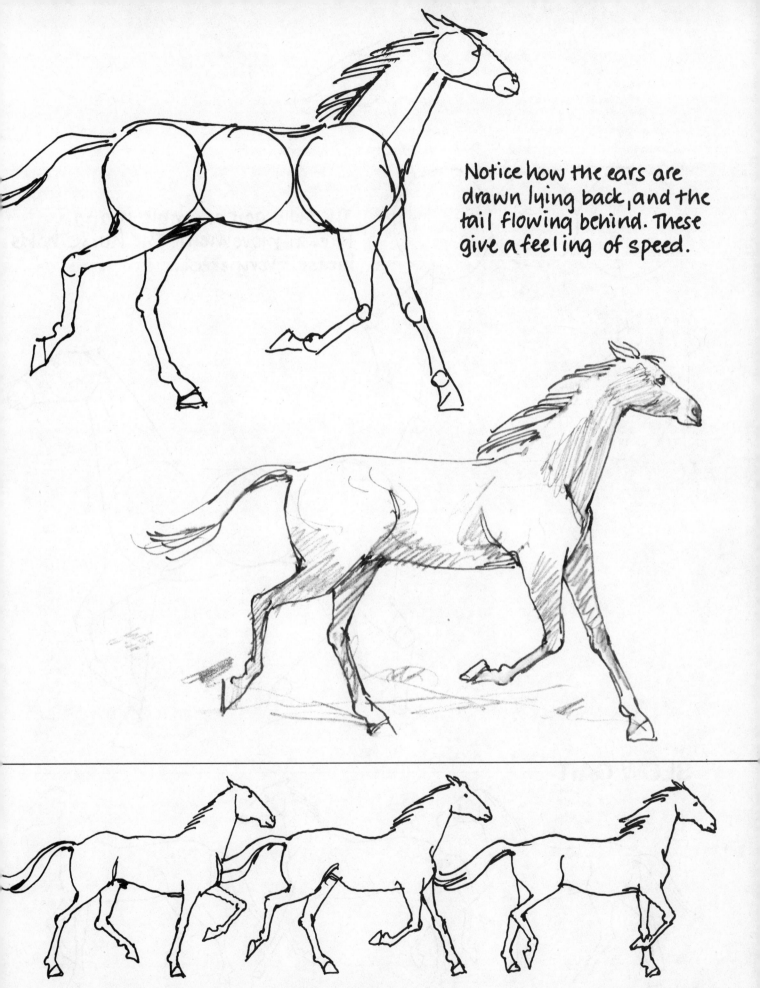

Notice how the ears are drawn lying back, and the tail flowing behind. These give a feeling of speed.

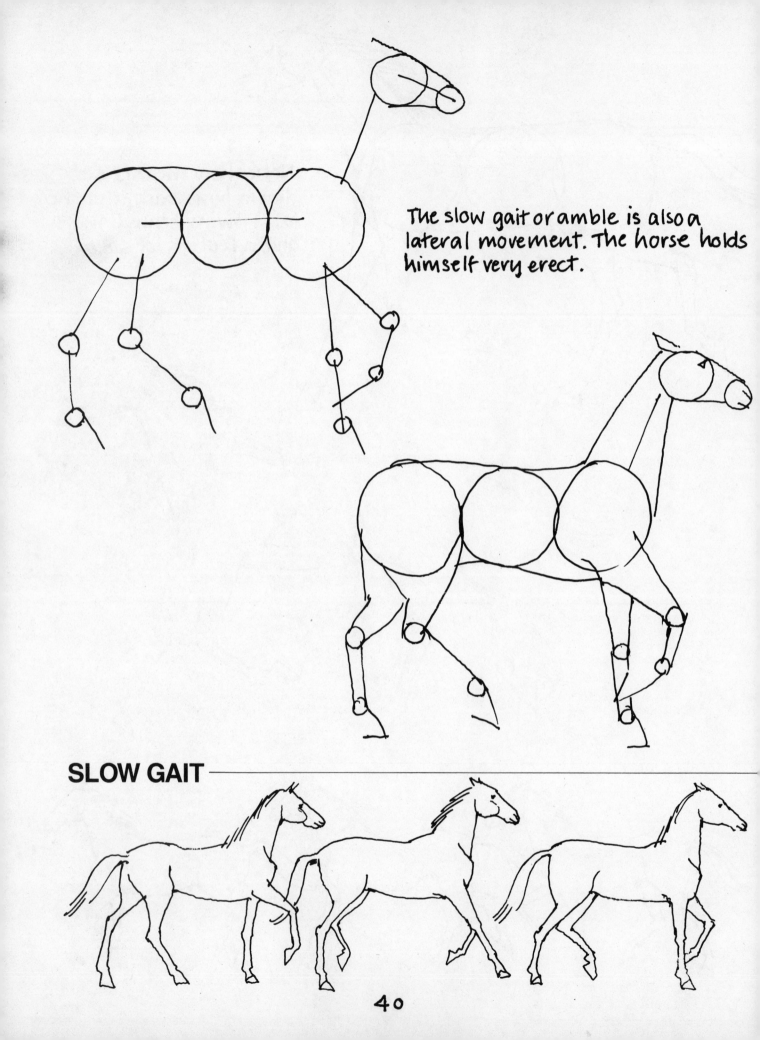

The slow gait or amble is also a lateral movement. The horse holds himself very erect.

SLOW GAIT

40

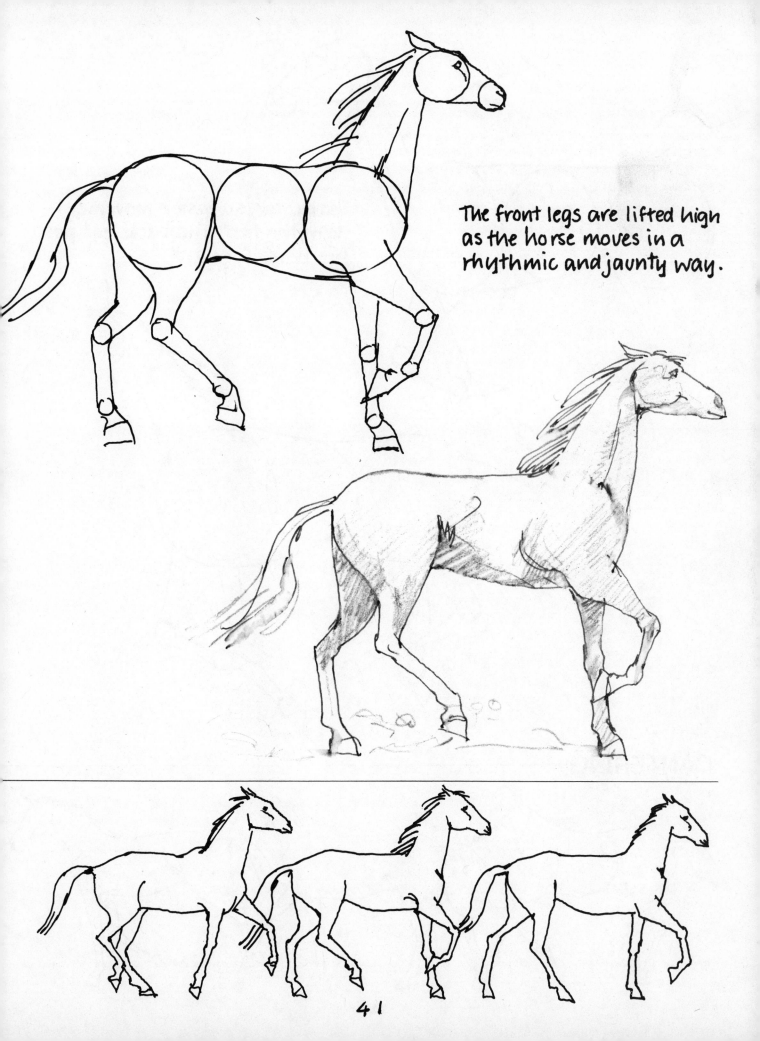

The front legs are lifted high as the horse moves in a rhythmic and jaunty way.

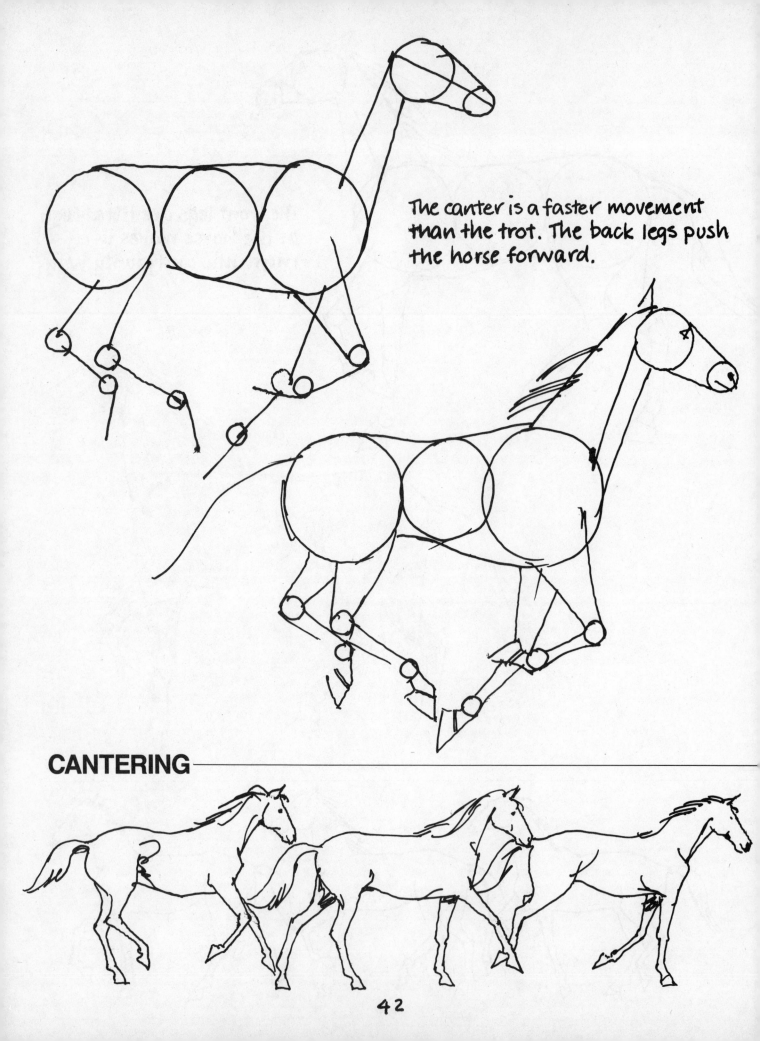

The canter is a faster movement than the trot. The back legs push the horse forward.

CANTERING

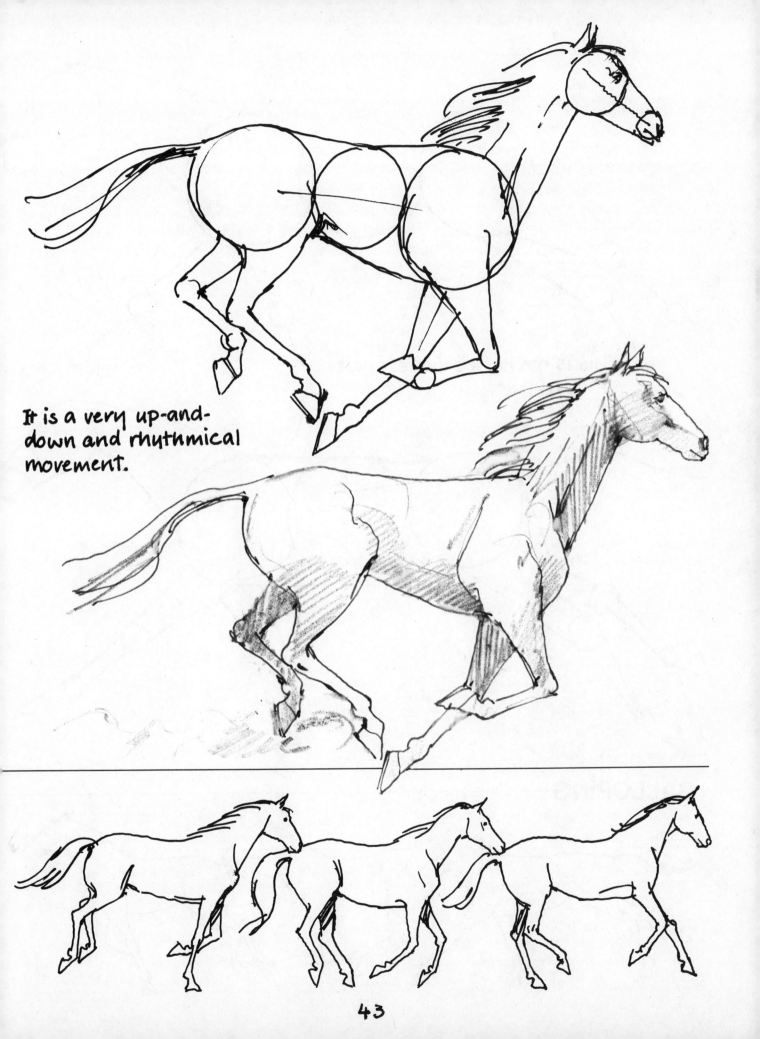

It is a very up-and-down and rhythmical movement.

43

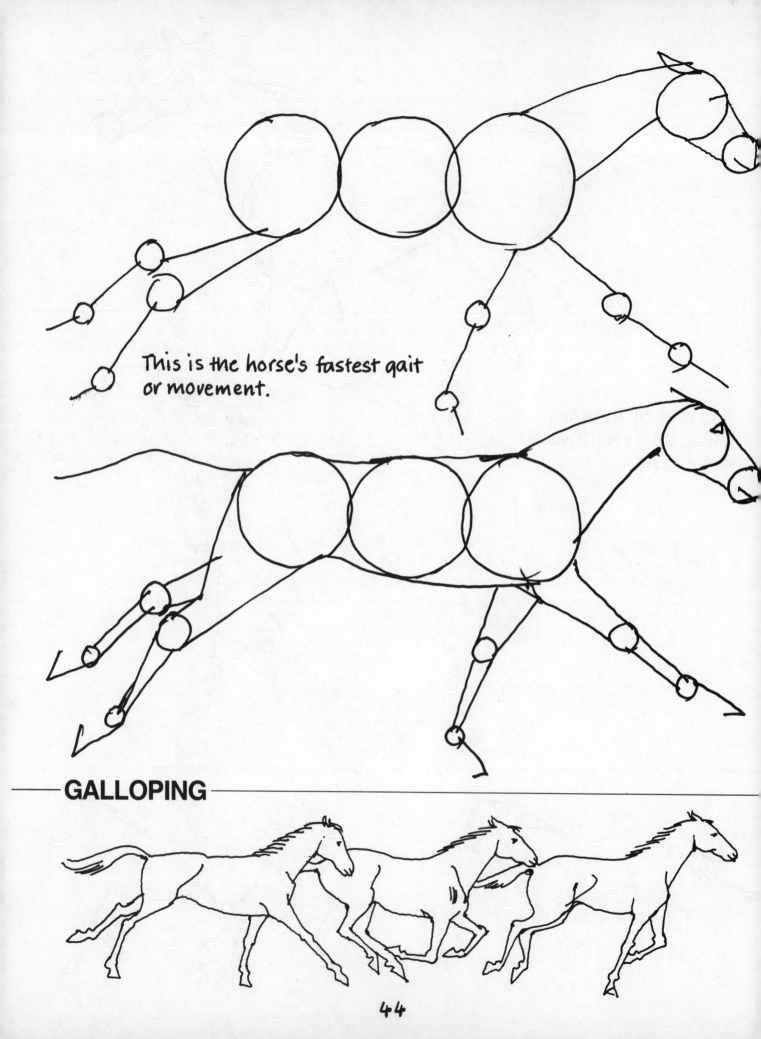

This is the horse's fastest gait or movement.

GALLOPING

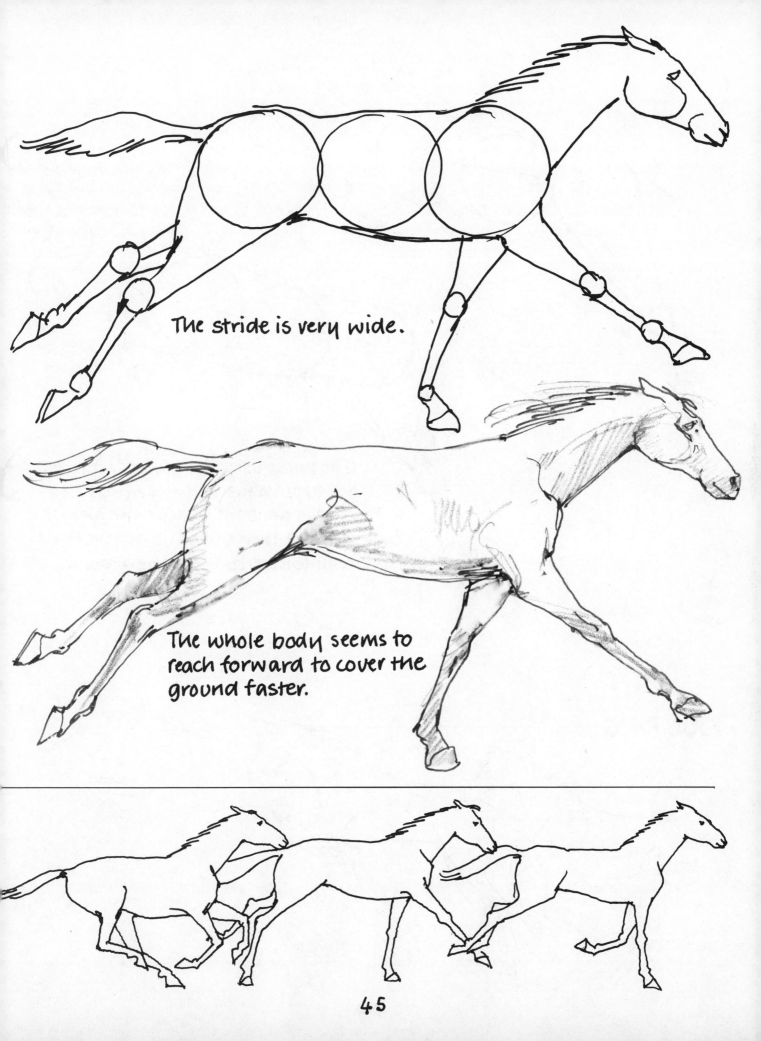

The stride is very wide.

The whole body seems to
reach forward to cover the
ground faster.

The horse uses the power in his rear legs to push his body upwards. The front legs are bent to clear the jump. The back legs are then pulled up as the front legs are unfolded to meet the ground.

JUMPING

The horse will land with one front leg slightly ahead of the other in order to gain his balance and keep moving quickly.

PULLING

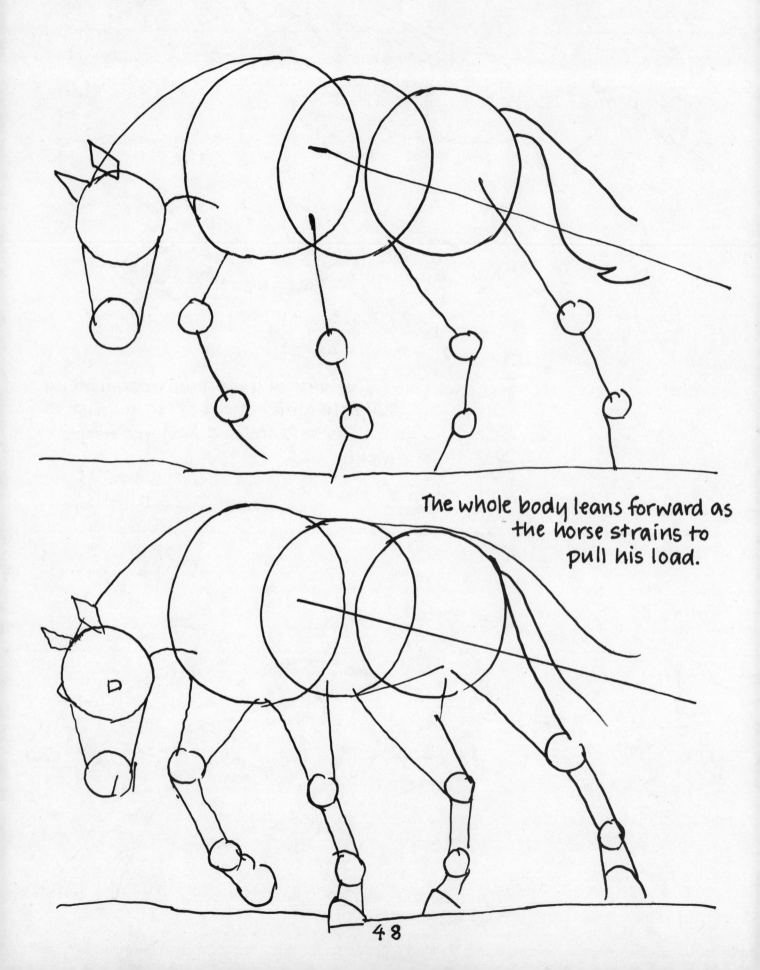

The whole body leans forward as the horse strains to pull his load.

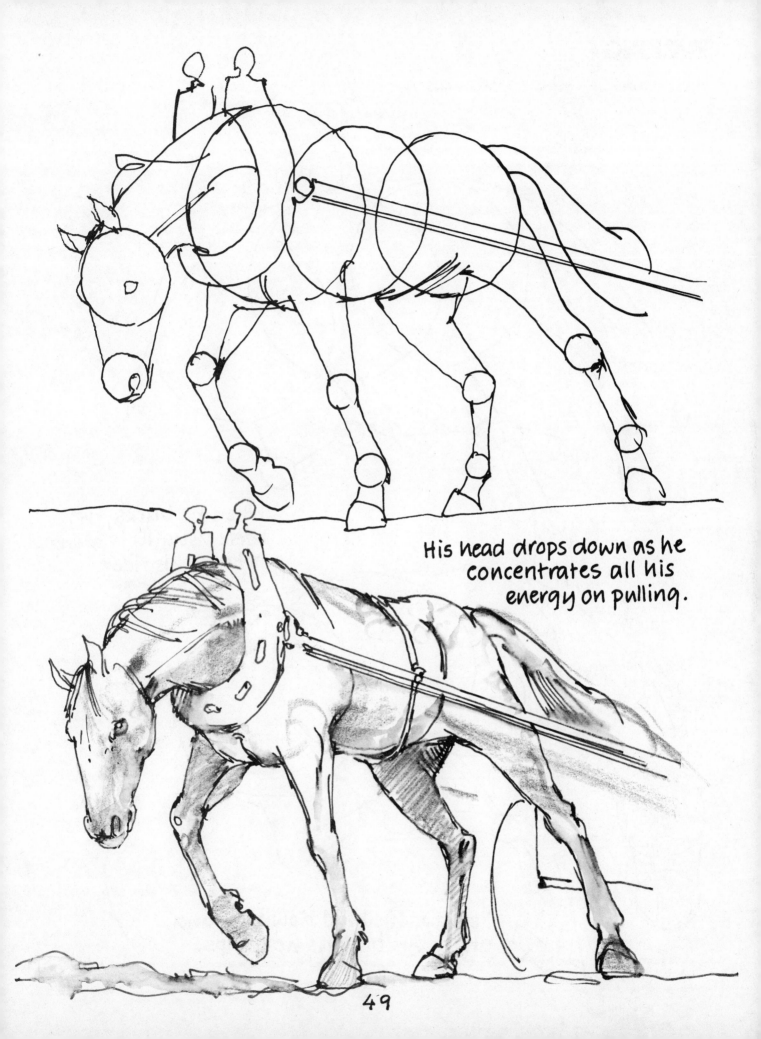

His head drops down as he
concentrates all his
energy on pulling.

49

BUCKING

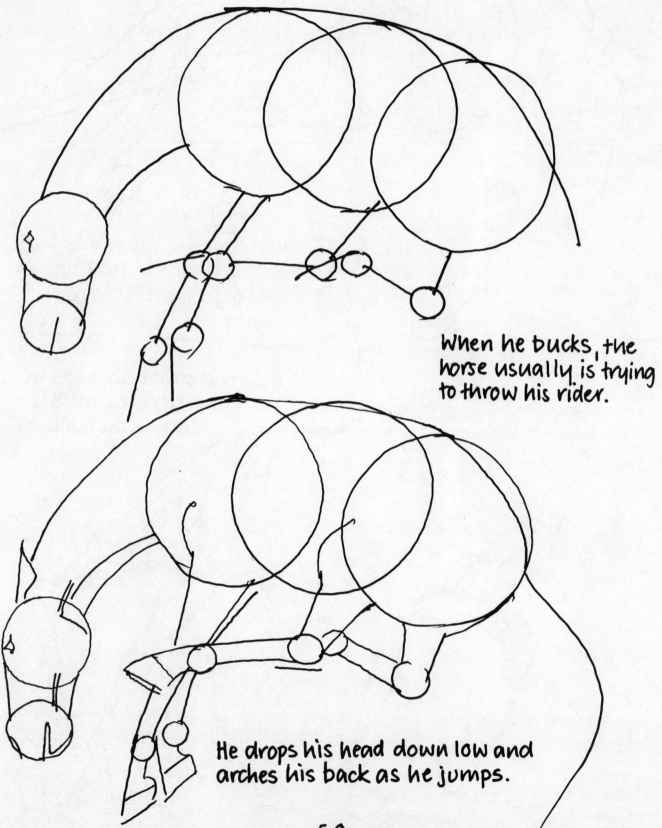

When he bucks, the horse usually is trying to throw his rider.

He drops his head down low and arches his back as he jumps.

51

REARING

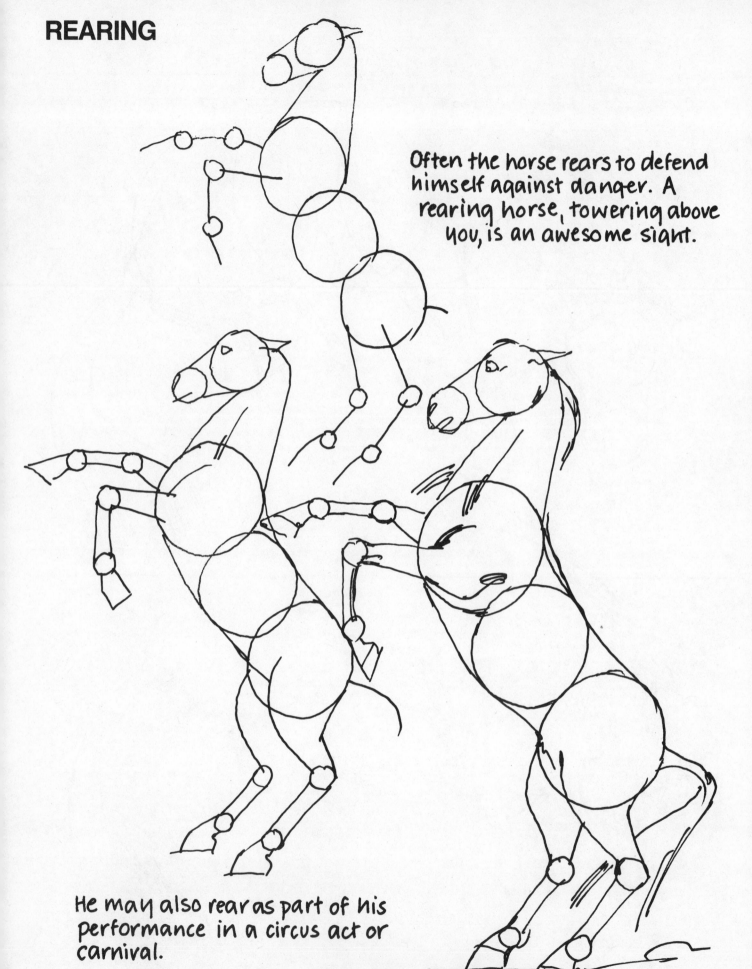

Often the horse rears to defend himself against danger. A rearing horse, towering above you, is an awesome sight.

He may also rear as part of his performance in a circus act or carnival.

Notice how much white
of the eye shows when
the horse is frightened
enough to rear.

See how the back legs are bent
and positioned to support the
whole weight of the horse.

SHYING

A frightened horse will shy away from danger rather than rear. He turns his head towards whatever has startled him and pulls his body away from it.

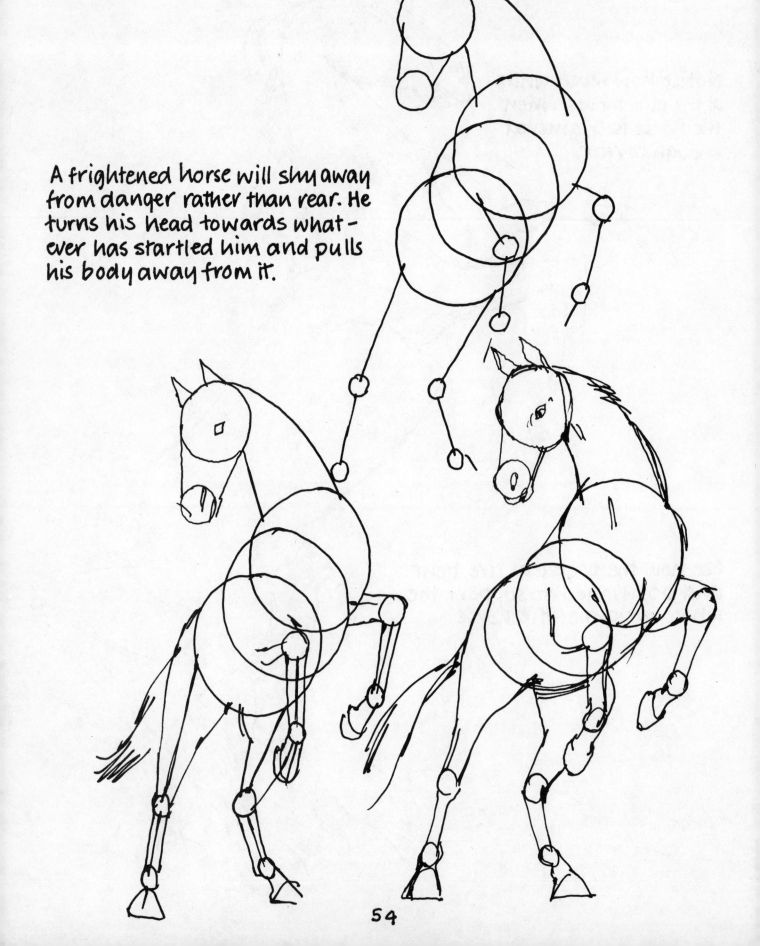

A shying horse will sometimes
raise himself up on his back legs
but does not look as aggressive
as a rearing horse.

BREEDS OF HORSES AND PONIES

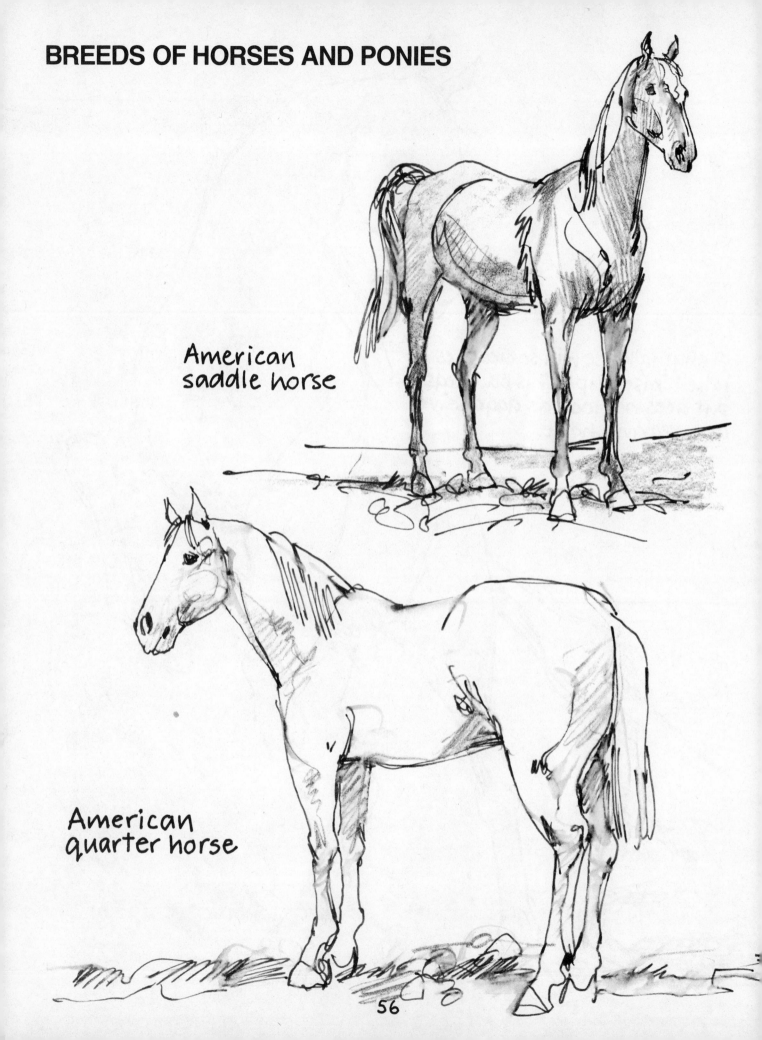

American
saddle horse

American
quarter horse

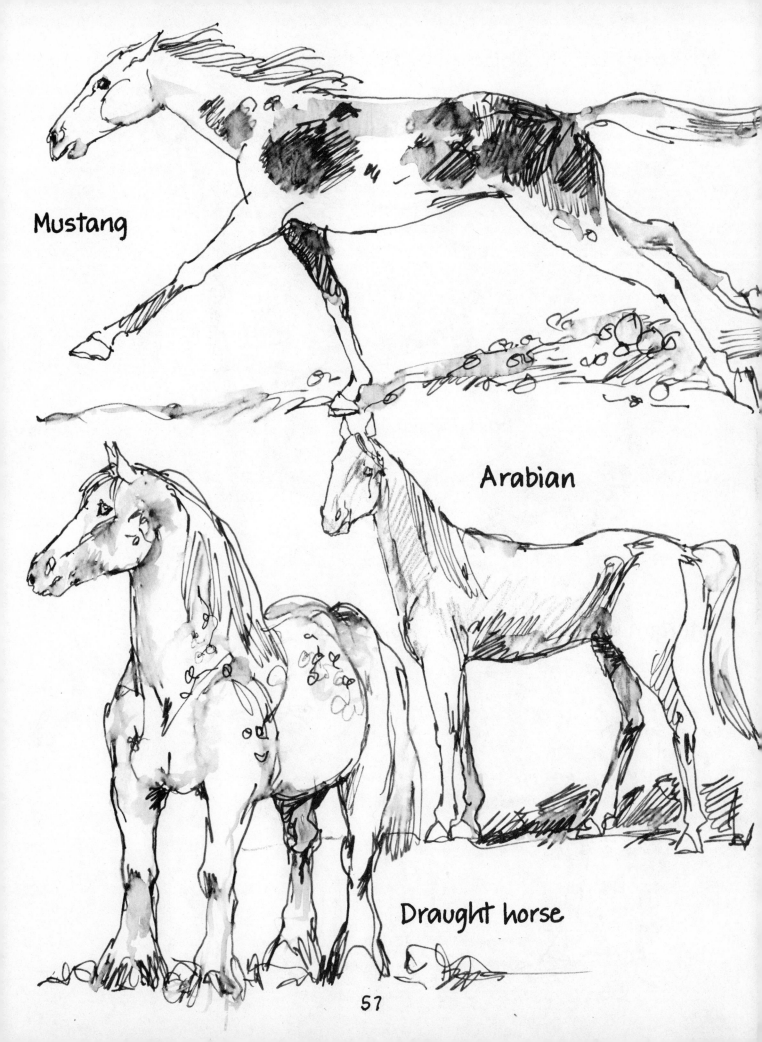

Mustang

Arabian

Draught horse

Pinto.

Morgan mare and foal.

Palomino pony.

Andalusian

Shetland pony.

Appaloosa

59

ASSEMBLING THE ACTION MODEL

You will find all the pieces you need to make up the model on the back cover of this book. If you feel it is a shame to spoil your book, trace the shapes and paste them on to stiff, thin cardboard.

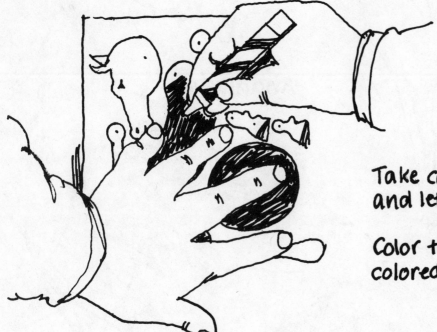

Take care to mark all the dots and letters in the correct places.

Color the horse with crayon or colored marker.

Cut out the pieces carefully with sharp scissors.

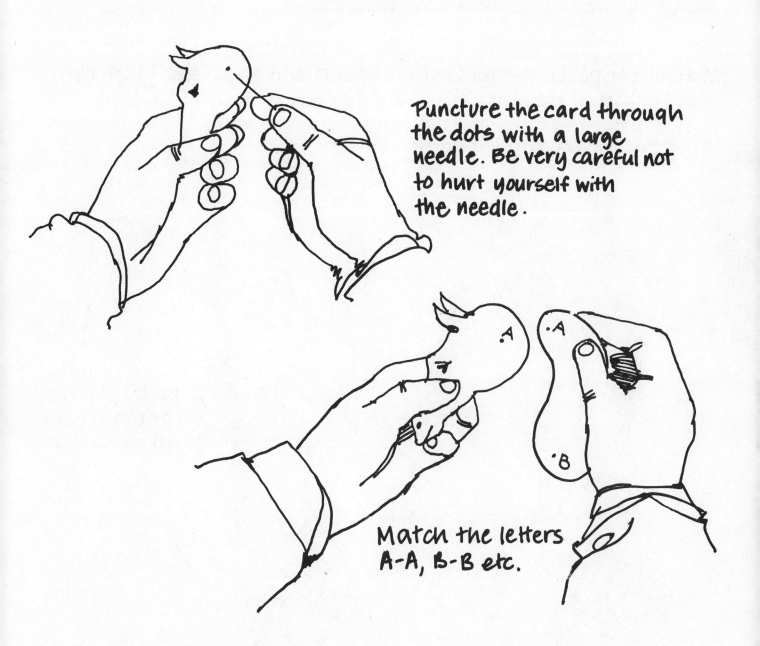

Puncture the card through the dots with a large needle. Be very careful not to hurt yourself with the needle.

Match the letters A-A, B-B etc.

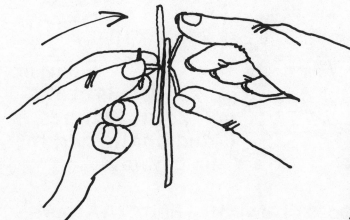

Use paper fasteners to join the pieces together.

Watch out for the place where the legs meet the body. Three pieces come together at this point.

HOW TO USE THE ACTION MODEL

Adjust the paper fasteners until the parts will move freely but will still stay in place when you have fixed a pose.

Move the model into the chosen pose.

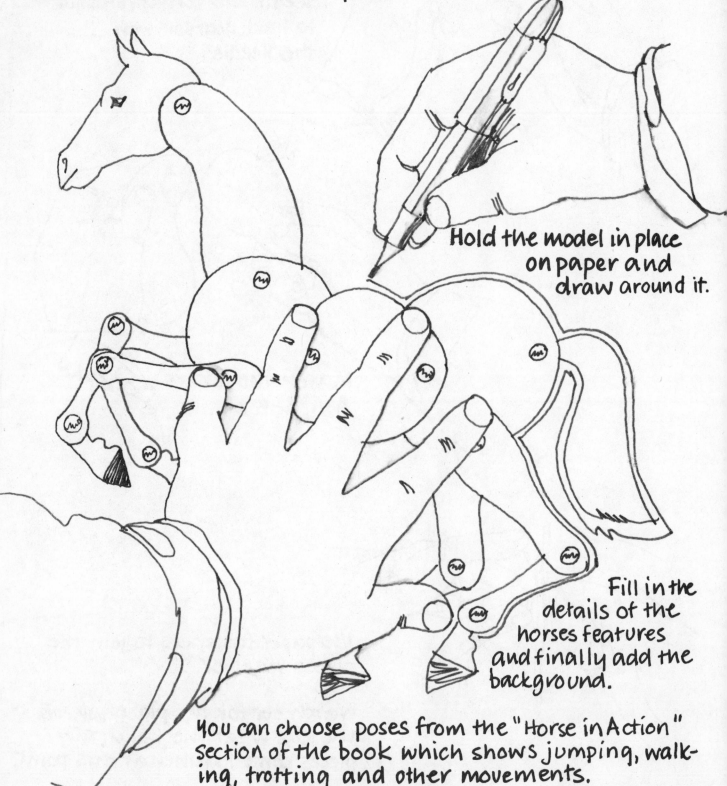

Hold the model in place on paper and draw around it.

Fill in the details of the horses features and finally add the background.

You can choose poses from the "Horse in Action" section of the book which shows jumping, walking, trotting and other movements.

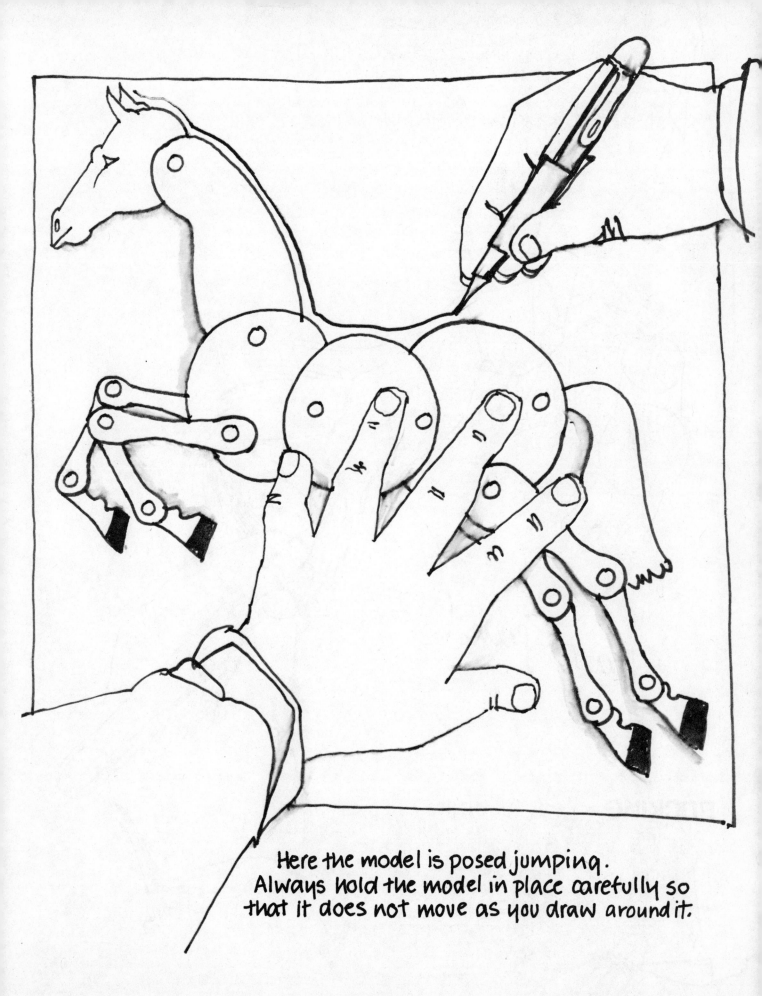

Here the model is posed jumping.
Always hold the model in place carefully so
that it does not move as you draw around it.

Have fun!